Barbara Hayes
Illustrated by Mary Brooks

Talking to God

CHILDREN'S PRAYERS for SPECIAL OCCASIONS

DEAN

Mother's Day

Dear Father in Heaven,

Today is Mother's day, when I thank dear Mummy for looking after me. Thank You, my Father in Heaven for the wonderful gift of a mother. Help me to thank her for her patience and kindness. Please bless the gift I give her today. Please never let me make her sad. In my good fortune, do not let me forget those children whose mothers cannot be with them. Please look down on them with special kindness, so that they may know they are not alone, but surrounded by the love of their heavenly Father.

Your loving child ─────────────

Helping Mummy and Learning to Help God

Dear Father in Heaven,

Today I have been helping Mummy. There is always plenty of work to do about the house. The grown-ups tell me that there is always plenty of God's work to be done, too. They say that when I am kind and good and help others, I am doing God's work. Dear Father in Heaven, please help me to do Your work all my life.

Your loving child _____

A Child's Prayer at Easter

Dear Father in Heaven,

Once more I kneel and thank You for all the blessings of this world. Most of all I thank You for sending Your beloved son, Jesus, to live and die for us and to save us from our sins. Thank You for the stories He told and the lessons He taught. Thank You for the example of His life, which showed us all how we should live. Please bless all children and let them always follow the teachings of Jesus.

Your loving child ———————

Ascension Day

Dear Father in Heaven,

I know that today is Ascension Day, and that it is a happy day. It is the day when, after much sorrow, Your dear son, Jesus, rose up and joined You in heaven. Please help me to understand that some days will be sad days, but that many days will be happy ones. For Jesus' sake, comfort me and all children on the sad days and help us to share our joy with others on the happy days.

Your loving child _____

A Prayer for Forgiveness

Dear Father in Heaven,

Tonight I kneel and pray for forgiveness. I did not mean to be naughty. I did not know I was being naughty. I did not feel as if I was. I thought I was having fun. However, now I know that what seems like a game to me can make extra work for other people. And I know that games which become too rough can end with someone being hurt.

Dear Lord, please help me to be sensible in the things I do. Teach me to tell right from wrong, but if I do still make mistakes, forgive me and help other people to forgive me, too.

Your loving child _____

Summer Holidays

Dear Father in Heaven,

Today I say my prayers to thank You for all happy summer holidays. Thank You for the good times we had at the sea. Thank You for the hot days, and the pretty flowers out in the countryside. Thank You for all the games we played.

Please bless our dear mothers and fathers who take us on holiday. Please look down with love on all the engine drivers, railway workers, and airline pilots, and shopkeepers and ice-cream sellers and everyone who works to make summer holidays possible. Dear Lord thank You for all these kind people.

Your loving child ─────────────

Mother's Birthday

Dear Father in Heaven,

I kneel to pray today to ask Your help in doing very important things. Today is the birthday of dear Mummy. Please help me to be good and make this day a happy one. My best present to Mummy will be a hug and a kiss to show how much I love her. Thank You, God, for the blessing of my family about me. Bless those children who have no family. Keep them safe and happy. Let them one day find people who will love and care for them as their own Mothers and Fathers would.

Your loving child ─────────

A New Baby

Dear Father in Heaven,

Thank You for the gift of the dear, new baby, which has come to live with us in our home. His eyes are so big and trusting. Thank You for his hands which clutch at mine. Thank You for his sweet smiles. Please help me to look after him and teach him to be good.

Our new baby is safe and warm. Please also bless all new babies born into the world.

Your loving child ─────────

A Pet's Birthday

Dear Father in Heaven,

I kneel to pray today to ask You to bless my pet on his birthday. I know my pet is little and unimportant, but he means a lot to me. Mummy and Daddy tell me that You love every creature on earth, even the smallest sparrow. Please understand then, dear Father, when I ask You, amidst all the important things You do, to find time to bless my little pet and keep him safe.

Thank You for all pets — kittens, puppies, hamsters, goldfish, bunnies, ponies and any others, whose names I know You will never forget, even if I do.

Your loving child ——————

A Prayer on Father's Day

Dear Father in Heaven,

I say my prayers today to thank You for my dear father who works so hard to look after me and our family. On this day, which is Father's Day, help me to be good and show Daddy how much I love him. Teach me the proper way to help Daddy about the house and in the garden, for I know that helping him shows how much I care.

Please bless Daddy and keep him safe while he is away at work, and whenever he is travelling. Please look after all fathers the whole world over, and bring them safely home.

Your loving child ───────

A Prayer on Christmas Day

Dear Father in Heaven,

I know that today I must say a special prayer because today is the day on which Your dearly beloved son was born. I think of Mary and Joseph and the baby Jesus in the stable at Bethlehem. I think of the three Wise Men and the shepherds gathered round the crib. Thank You for sending the holy baby to save us.

Today I will say my prayers and remember the true meaning of Christmas, then please bless me while I enjoy this special day. Please make Christmas happy for everyone.

Your loving child ——

New Year's Day

Dear Father in Heaven,

I kneel to pray on this New Year's Day to thank You for bringing me safely to the beginning of another year. Thank You for all the beautiful things I have seen in the last twelve months, the blue skies and the trees and the flowers, the white snow and the clouds and the autumn leaves. Thank You for the people who have looked after me and the friends who have played with me. Thank You for all my food and clothes. Thank You for my toys and my pets. Dear God, please bless me in the year ahead. Keep me safe and good, that I may grow up to help and comfort others as they have cared for me.

Your loving child ——————